Letts

KS2 Success

Age 7-9

Grammar & punctuation

Practice workbook

Laura Griffiths

About this book

Grammar and punctuation

Grammar and punctuation are a key focus of the new primary curriculum. They are crucial English skills that will enable your child to communicate effectively in school and in later life. Developing these skills will help your child to convey clear and accurate information when speaking and writing.

This book separates grammar from punctuation and breaks them down topic by topic, offering clear explanations and practice at each step. It will also aid preparation for the Key Stage 2 **English Grammar, Punctuation and Spelling** test.

Features of the book

- The *Key to grammar* and *Key to punctuation* sections introduce each topic through concise explanations and clear examples.

- *Practice activities* include a variety of tasks to see how well your child has grasped each concept.

- *Test your grammar* and *Test your punctuation* provide focused questions after both sections.

- A *mixed test* at the end of the book helps to cement your child's overall understanding of the grammar and punctuation topics covered.

- *Answers* are in a pull-out booklet at the centre of the book.

Grammar and punctuation tips

- Spend time reading and looking through books (both fiction and non-fiction) asking your child to identify examples of different types of grammar and punctuation. For example, play 'finding an adjective' or 'spotting speech marks', or talk about why a new paragraph has started.

- Encourage your child to write by making diaries, recipe cards, stories and letters together. Encourage them to use the correct punctuation in their own writing.

- Make grammar and punctuation fun. For example, play games like *I spy* but start with: 'I am thinking of a noun beginning with…' or a charades-type game where your child can act out an adverb.

Contents

Grammar

Alphabetical order	**4**
What is a sentence?	**6**
Verbs	**8**
Nouns	**10**
Nouns – singular and plural	**12**
Proper and collective nouns	**14**
Phrases	**16**
Clauses	**18**
Pronouns	**20**
Verbs – which tense?	**22**
Future tense	**24**
Irregular verbs	**26**
Was or were?	**28**
Did or done?	**30**
Prepositions	**32**
Adjectives 1	**34**
Adjectives 2	**36**
Adverbs 1	**38**
Adverbs 2	**40**
Determiners	**42**
Conjunctions	**44**
Time connectives	**46**
Test your grammar	**48**

Punctuation

Full stops	**50**
Exclamation marks	**52**
Question marks	**54**
Capital letters	**56**
Commas in a list	**58**
Direct speech 1	**60**
Direct speech 2	**62**
Paragraphs	**64**
Test your punctuation	**66**

Mixed practice questions

Mixed test	**68**

Answers

Answers (centre pull-out)	**1–8**

Alphabetical order

Key to grammar

There are 26 letters in the alphabet:

a b c d e f g h i j k l m n o p q r s t u v w x y z

The vowels are **a**, **e**, **i**, **o** and **u**. The remaining letters are **consonants**.

Sometimes words need to be put into **alphabetical order** (for instance, last names in a class register). To do this you need to look at the first letter of each word.

cat   **d**og   **m**ouse

If there are two words with the same first letter, the second letter is used, then the next one, and so on.

cat   **co**w   **do**g   **du**ck

Practice activities

1. Fill in the missing letters in the alphabet.

    a) a _____ c d e _____ g h i j _____ l m n _____ p q _____ s t u v

        _____ x _____ _____

    b) f g _____ i j k _____

    c) _____ _____ _____ _____ z

2. Look at the pictures. Write them in alphabetical order on the line below.

aeroplane

train

bus

car

_____

3. Look at the lists of words. Rewrite them in alphabetical order.

a) football, tennis, cricket, swimming

_____

b) cheese, ham, tuna, jam, egg

_____

c) shorts, trousers, skirt, vest, jacket, shoes

_____

What is a sentence?

Key to grammar

A sentence is a sequence of words that makes sense.

A sentence usually has a **subject** (generally something or someone who is doing something) and a **verb** (a doing or being word).

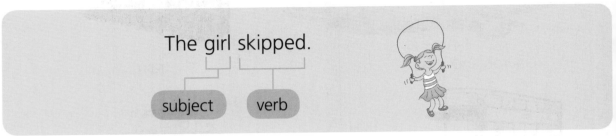

The girl skipped.

subject   verb

Sentences can be made longer by adding more detail or linking sentences using joining words.

There are different types of sentence:

Type	Definition	End punctuation
Statement	A sentence that gives information.	full stop (.)
Question	A sentence that needs an answer.	question mark (?)
Exclamation	A sentence that shows an emotion.	exclamation mark (!)
Command	A sentence that tells someone to do something.	full stop (.) or exclamation mark (!)

Practice activities

1. Put one tick in each row to show whether the sentence is a statement or a question.

Sentence	Statement	Question
a) What would you like for dinner today?		
b) I can count to 100.		
c) Did you enjoy your birthday party?		
d) The dog barked so loudly, he woke us up.		

2. Rewrite these sentences putting the words in the correct order so they make sense.

a) The car red was.

_____

b) Have you started book reading your?

_____

c) quiet Be!

_____

d) like I eating jam toast with on top.

_____

3. Look at each sentence below and write whether it is a statement, question or command.

a) When is your birthday?   _____

b) A square has four straight sides.   _____

c) Go away!   _____

d) The weather forecast is for rain tomorrow.   _____

e) Where are you going on holiday?   _____

f) Come back here!   _____

g) Wait there!   _____

h) I think I like it.   _____

i) Did he play well?   _____

j) My favourite fruit is oranges.   _____

Verbs

Key to grammar

A verb is a **doing** or a **being** word. It usually describes an action. It tells us what is happening or what will or has happened.

Examples: eat, walk, learn, swim, laugh

Practice activities

1. Look at the pictures and write the verb each picture is showing.

    a)

    _____

    b)

    _____

    c)

    _____

    d)

    _____

2. Underline the verb in each sentence.

    a) Mrs Jones cooks tasty meals.

    b) Cinderella dances with Prince Charming at the ball.

    c) The shop sells lots of clothes.

    d) My brother listens to his music on the computer.

3. Circle all the verbs.

eat   sleep   stretch   orange

climb   tail

jump   drink

          ears   food   pounce

4. Write three verbs to show what each animal below can do.

a)

_____
_____
_____

b)

_____
_____
_____

c)

_____
_____
_____

d)

_____
_____
_____

Nouns

Key to grammar

A **noun** is a word used to refer to a person, animal, place or thing.

Common nouns are general words for people, animals, places and things.

They are not their names but words that tell us what they are.

They do not begin with a capital letter, unless they begin a sentence.

man	girl	dog	horse	station	
hotel	planet	chair	pencil	moon	

Practice activities

1. Look at the pictures and write the common noun.

a)

_____

b)

_____

c)

_____

d)

_____

2. Circle the common noun in each sentence.

    a) The bird flew away.

    b) We are at the airport.

    c) I brushed my teeth.

    d) The girl jumped high.

3. Circle **all** the common nouns in each sentence.

    a) She wiped the table with the dirty cloth.

    b) Sarah went to the shops and bought some bread and milk.

    c) Alex washed the car and used a bucket, water and two sponges.

    d) The boys played cricket in the park after school.

    e) Their mum asked them to tidy their bedrooms because there were too many toys on the floor.

    f) He licked the ice cream before it melted.

4. Choose a common noun from the box below to fill in the gaps in the sentences.

beach	school	teacher
sweets	monkey	
bag		shells

    a) The cheeky _____ ate all the bananas.

    b) The sandy _____ was covered with _____.

    c) This morning I was late for _____ and forgot my

    _____.

    d) Our _____ likes eating _____.

5. Write your own sentence that includes **two** common nouns.

_____

_____

Nouns – singular and plural

Key to grammar

Nouns can either be **singular** or **plural.** Singular means one. Plural means more than one.

A **regular** plural noun ends in **s** or **es**.

Sometimes a plural noun can be **irregular** and not end in **s** or **es**.

Regular			Irregular	
Singular	**Plural**		**Singular**	**Plural**
girl	girls		person	people
class	classes		man	men

An apostrophe is used to show possession of a singular or plural noun. This is when something belongs to someone or something.

Singular	**Plural**
The dog**'s** basket	The dogs**'** basket

Practice activities

1. Underline all the **plural** nouns in each sentence below.

   a) The cows were in the field.

   b) The excited astronauts were trying on their new spacesuits.

   c) We are going to the library to listen to stories.

   d) The cats and dogs were making lots of noise because they were frightened of the loud fireworks.

   e) We have sandwiches, crisps, apples and sweets in our picnic today.

   f) There were lots of people waiting at the platform for the next two trains this morning.

2. Write the **irregular plural** for each of these nouns.

a)

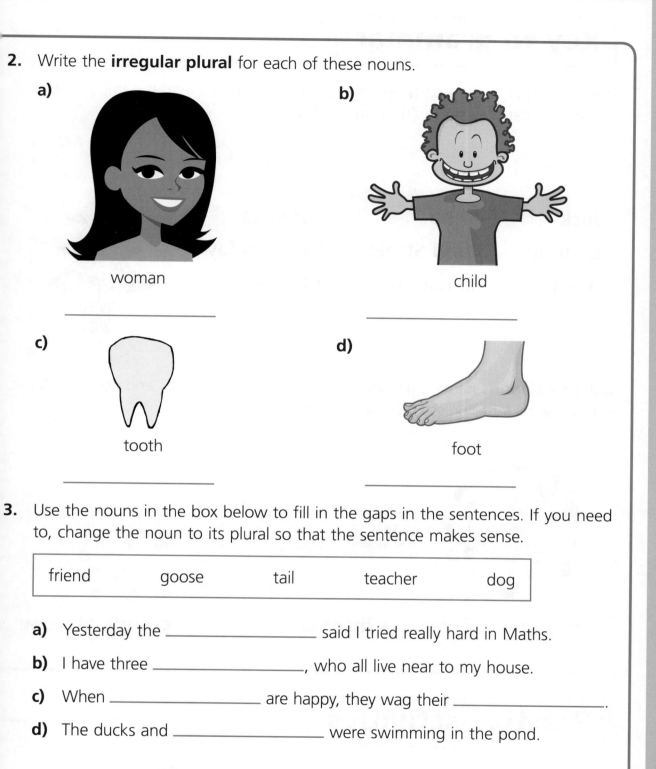

woman

_____

b)

child

_____

c)

tooth

_____

d)

foot

_____

3. Use the nouns in the box below to fill in the gaps in the sentences. If you need to, change the noun to its plural so that the sentence makes sense.

friend	goose	tail	teacher	dog

a) Yesterday the _____ said I tried really hard in Maths.

b) I have three _____, who all live near to my house.

c) When _____ are happy, they wag their _____.

d) The ducks and _____ were swimming in the pond.

Proper and collective nouns

Key to grammar

Proper nouns name a particular person, place, time or event. It is important to remember that they start with a **capital letter**.

Jack   Aisha   America
London   Bond Street   Wednesday
April   Ramadan   Christmas

Collective nouns name a **group** of people, animals or things and do not begin with a capital letter unless they begin a sentence.

a **group** of children   a **litter** of kittens   a **gaggle** of geese

Practice activities

1. Circle the words that are **proper nouns**.

   chocolate   Mrs Smith   April

   presents   Manchester   Max

2. Choose one of the proper nouns in the box below to add to each sentence.

| Cardiff | January | Sara |

a) My birthday is in _____.

b) _____ likes going to the cinema.

c) _____ is the capital city of Wales.

3. Draw lines to match each group of animals to the correct **collective noun**.

a)

herd

b)

swarm

c)

brood

d)

flock

Phrases

Key to grammar

A **phrase** is a small group of words that makes up a meaningful unit in a sentence.

A phrase does not usually have a verb and it does not make sense on its own.

The rubbish was put **in the bin**.

The fish were swimming **around the pond**.

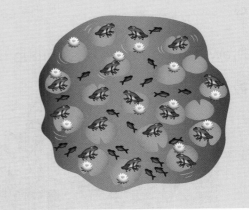

Often a single noun could replace a phrase. Phrases are used to add more detail.

The **lucky, little girl** won a prize.

This could simply have said, "The girl won a prize." The words "lucky, little" add more detail.

Practice activities

1. What word type is **not** usually found in phrases? Circle one.

   verb   noun   adjective   adverb

16

2. Underline the phrase in each of these sentences.

   a) My friend's cat likes jumping.

   b) We ate dinner in the kitchen.

   c) I drank a cup of warm tea.

   d) Alex ran along the beach.

   e) Kara's pink bedroom was messy.

   f) He walked down the path.

   g) We can't go shopping in the heavy rain.

3. Choose a phrase below to complete each of the sentences.

of dirty plates	at the park	after lunch
deep and cold	upside down	small and quiet

   a) Bats hang _____.

   b) The waiter was carrying a pile _____.

   c) The mouse, _____, scuttled away.

   d) The sea is _____.

   e) We played football _____.

   f) Bo finished his homework _____.

4. Read the phrase at the start of each sentence and write a suitable ending.

   a) After a long time, _____
   _____

   b) The pretty, white snowflakes _____
   _____

Clauses

Key to grammar

A **main clause** is a sequence of words creating a single idea that makes sense on its own.

It has a verb and a subject.

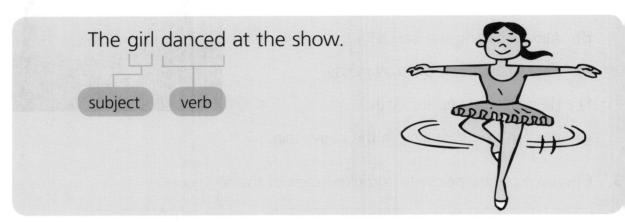

The girl danced at the show.

subject   verb

A **subordinate clause** is still one idea, but does **not** make sense on its own.
A subordinate clause needs a main clause. Together they make a **complex sentence**.

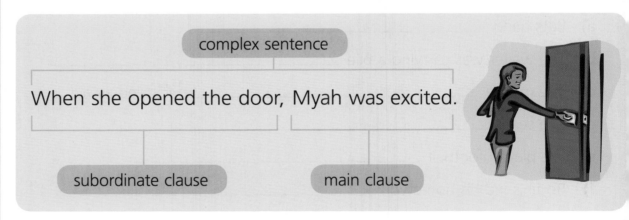

complex sentence

When she opened the door, Myah was excited.

subordinate clause   main clause

Subordinate clauses can start with words such as:

after	although	as
because	before	if
since	that	until
when	which	while	who

Practice activities

1. Choose the correct subordinate clause from the boxes below to fill in the gaps in the sentences.

| even though she had cried | | As her dinner was ready |

| because he was late |

   a) Eric ran out of the house quickly _____

   b) _____, Tilly opened the kitchen door and sat

   down at the table.

   c) The dentist gave the girl a sticker _____

2. Underline the **main** clause(s) in each sentence.

   a) When the teacher came into the room, we stopped talking.

   b) We went to the park because the sun was shining.

   c) I spent my pocket money, but my grandad gave me some extra money.

   d) Although they are very noisy, the drums are my favourite instrument.

3. Look at each picture and write a complex sentence for each one using a main clause and a subordinate clause.

   a)

   b)

   _____   _____

   _____   _____

   _____   _____

Pronouns

Key to grammar

A **pronoun** is a word that is used to replace a noun. Pronouns are often used so that the noun is not repeated and to make our writing more interesting.

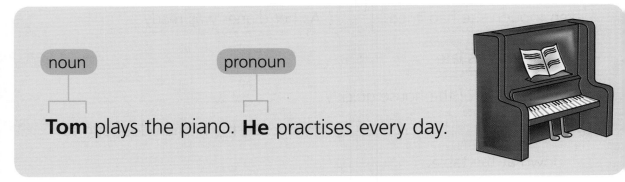

noun   pronoun

Tom plays the piano. **He** practises every day.

Some common pronouns are:

I, me, mine   it, its

you, yours   we, us, ours

he, him, his   they, them, theirs

she, her, hers

Practice activities

1. Put a circle around all the pronouns.

he	them	cat	Mrs
Matthew	walking	John	car
she	it	chair	I
house	Sophia	us	snake

Pronouns

2. Underline the pronouns in each sentence.

   a) Charlie was tired, so he went upstairs to bed.

   b) A spider crawled up the chair. It was large and black.

   c) Rebecca played with some toys while she was on holiday.

   d) Bethan doesn't eat many sweets because she knows they are bad for the teeth.

   e) The builder came, but we were out.

   f) "The ball is not yours. It is mine!" he shouted.

3. Use the pronouns below to complete the story extract.

I	them	they	you

An old man on the point of death called his sons to give them some advice. He told them to bring in a bundle of sticks, and said to the eldest son:

"Break it."

The son really strained but was unable to break the bundle. The other sons

tried too, but none of _____ could do it.

"Untie the bundle," said the father, "and each of _____ take a stick."

When _____ each had a stick, he said to them:

"Now, break them," and each stick broke easily.

Their father then asked: "You see what _____ mean?"

4. Rewrite the sentence replacing the words in bold with a pronoun.

Dexter read a long book even though **Dexter** found **the long book** difficult.

_____

_____

21

Verbs – which tense?

Key to grammar

A **verb** is a doing or being word. Verbs change with different tenses.
- The **past tense** describes something that has already happened.
- The **present tense** is what is happening now.
- The **future tense** refers to what will happen in the future.
- The **present perfect tense** describes something that began in the past but was completed in the present (using the present tense of the verb 'have').

Verb	Present	Past	Future	Present perfect
jump	I jump	I jumped	I will jump	I have jumped

Practice activities

1. Underline the verb(s) in each sentence.

   a) Toby shouted at his brother.

   b) The monkey grabbed a large bunch of bananas.

   c) The children will eat their dinner in the hall.

   d) We are riding our bikes to the park.

   e) Emma and Tina danced at the disco last night.

   f) I drink water because it keeps me healthy.

   g) Charlotte cried when she fell off her scooter.

Verbs – which tense?

2. Fill in the gaps in the table to show how each verb changes tense.

Verb	Present	Past	Future
laugh	she laughs	she laughed	she will laugh
walk		you walked	you will walk
play	he plays		
talk		we talked	
skip	they skip		they will skip

3. Write these sentences again, changing the verbs so that they are in the **past tense.**

a) I work hard at school.

_____

b) I tidy my bedroom.

_____

c) We jump in muddy puddles.

_____

d) I play with my toys.

_____

4. Circle the correct form of the verb in the following sentences, which use the **present perfect tense**.

a) He **has / have** celebrated his birthday.

b) We have **open / opened** our presents.

c) I **has / have** blown out the candles.

23

Future tense

Key to grammar

The **future tense** tells us about things that will happen in the future.

When verbs are written in the future tense, we often add **will** or **shall** before the verb.

I **will** sing in the concert.

I **shall** run in the race.

Practice activities

1. Underline the verbs paired with **will** or **shall** in each sentence.

   a) The sports day will start at four o'clock.

   b) The girls will play football tomorrow.

   c) Next week, I shall walk to school.

   d) Tomorrow, I will run to school.

2. Fill in the gaps in the table using **will**.

Present tense	Future tense
I eat.	I will eat.
We cook.	
They sit.	

3. Some friends are going on holiday next week. Look at the pictures of everything they will do and write a sentence for each in the future tense.

a)

_____

b)

c)

_____

d)

_____

4. Circle the correct form of the verb for each sentence.

a) On holiday, I will **play** / **played** on the beach.

b) I will **ate** / **eat** my dinner in the kitchen.

c) The boys in my class will **learnt** / **learn** to play cricket.

d) My sister will **take** / **took** her exams next month.

e) The clown will **juggle** / **juggles** ten balls.

f) The whales will **dove** / **dive** soon.

Irregular verbs

Key to grammar

Most verbs are **regular** and can be changed easily from the present to the past tense by doing little more than adding **ed**.

Present tense	Past tense
I walk	I walk**ed**
I laugh	I laugh**ed**
I open	I open**ed**

Other verbs are **irregular** and don't follow this rule.

Present tense	Past tense
I am	I was
I speak	I spoke
I eat	I ate

Practice activities

1. Draw a line to match the correct present and past tense verb.

   a) break   heard

   b) know   did

   c) go   swam

   d) ride   took

   e) do   rode

   f) take   went

   g) swim   knew

   h) hear   broke

2. Circle the correct form of the verb, making sure that each sentence is in the **past** tense.

   a) The aeroplane **flies / flew** very high.

   b) The monkey **have / had** five bananas.

   c) Jack **sold / sell** the cow for some magic beans.

   d) The beanstalk **grow / grew** very high.

   e) The magician, outside the circus, **stood / stands** very still.

   f) The boy **sat / sit** on the chair.

3. Write the verbs in the correct tense to complete this table.

Present tense	Past tense
think	thought
	grew
find	
make	
	said
	blew

4. Choose one of the verbs from the table above and use it to write a sentence in the past tense.

_____

_____

5. Circle the words below to which **ed** can be added.

   play   **drive**   **cook**   **teach**

Was or were?

Key to grammar

Most mistakes in grammar are because the verb and the noun are not matched correctly.

For instance, sometimes **was** and **were** get muddled.

As a rule, if the subject is **singular** use **was,** except when the subject is **you**.

If the subject is **plural**, or the word **you** is used, put **were**.

Singular	Plural	You (singular or plural)
He **was** happy.	They **were** happy.	You [the boy] **were** happy.
The boy **was** happy.	The boys **were** happy.	You [the boys] **were** happy.

Practice activities

1. Complete these sentences using **was** or **were**.

   a) Rebecca and Varsha _____ baking a cake.

   b) The school gate _____ locked.

   c) The wicked witch _____ nasty to the frog.

   d) You _____ very cross!

   e) The cars _____ stuck in a traffic jam.

   f) It _____ her ballet exam last week.

2. Write **was** or **were** in the gaps so the story is written correctly.

Once upon a time, there _____ a lion lying by a tree. A little

mouse _____ running up and down the lion's back, and he

_____ beginning to make the lion angry. The lion turned its

large head and opened its mouth widely. With its piercing eyes glaring, the

lion _____ about to swallow the little mouse in one big gulp.

Just then, the little mouse squeaked, "Please don't eat me! One day you might

need me to help you."

The lion laughed but let the little mouse go free. He _____

sure he would never need help from such a small, pathetic creature. Then,

one day, three men _____ walking through the forest holding

nets. The men _____ trying to catch the lion and swiftly threw

a net over the lion's strong body. The lion roared and struggled, but there

_____ nothing he could do. He could not escape.

Just then, the little mouse returned to help the lion. He began, very slowly,

to gnaw and chew through the net with his sharp teeth. Eventually, the mouse

made a hole that _____ wide enough for the lion to escape.

3. Put a circle around the correct word to start each question.

a) **Was / Were** the girls playing tennis last night?

b) **Was / Were** it cold on the way to school this morning?

c) **Was / Were** there any sweets left in the bag?

d) **Was / Were** the television left on?

Did or done?

Key to grammar

Sometimes **did** and **done** get muddled. The words **has**, **have** or **had** should normally appear before **done**. The examples in the table below should help you.

Past tense	Present perfect tense	Past perfect tense
I **did** it.	I **have done** it.	I **had done** it.
You **did** it.	You **have done** it.	You **had done** it.
He/she/it **did** it.	He/she/it **has done** it.	He/she/it **had done** it.
We **did** it.	We **have done** it.	We **had done** it.
They **did** it.	They **have done** it.	They **had done** it.

Practice activities

1. In each sentence circle the correct form of the verb.

    a) They **done** / **did** it together.

    b) Ella had **did** / **done** very well in her badminton match.

    c) I **did** / **done** all my homework.

    d) They **done** / **did** the cooking together.

2. Write **did** or **done** in the following sentences

a) What _____ you buy from the shops?

b) They've _____ very well.

c) We've _____ the painting carefully.

d) _____ you catch the bus or the train?

e) We've _____ all our activities.

f) I _____ my best!

3. Draw a line to match the correct ending to the start of each sentence.

a) I have done   very well in their swimming lesson.

b) We did   a handstand together.

c) They did   nothing wrong!

4. Write two sentences of your own using **did** and **done** correctly.

a) _____

_____

b) _____

_____

Prepositions

Key to grammar

Prepositions are words that describe the relationship between one thing and another. They link nouns or pronouns to other words in a sentence.

> The dog is **in** his basket.
>
> The dog is **next to** the cat.
>
> The dog is **under** his blanket.

Prepositions show the relationship between things in terms of **place** or **time**.

> My dad laughed **during** the show.
>
> (*time*)

> My dad walked **over** the bridge.
>
> (*place*)

Practice activities

1. Underline the preposition in each sentence.

   a) The dirty, old dog ran into the house.

   b) Jessica sat next to her friend.

   c) Sam jumped in muddy puddles.

   d) The football team ran around the pitch.

   e) The ant is under the rock.

2. Put a circle around the prepositions below.

   under   after   blue   over

          on   girls   below   sun

3. Look at each picture and write a sentence using a preposition to describe it.

a)

_____

_____

_____

b)

_____

_____

_____

c)

_____

_____

_____

d)

_____

_____

_____

4. Circle one preposition to make each sentence correct.

a) I need to post the letter **into** / **onto** the postbox.

b) Suzie lives **around** / **next to** the park.

c) In English, Amy sits **behind** / **inside** me.

d) The boy hit the cricket ball **out of** / **over** the fence.

Adjectives 1

Key to grammar

Adjectives tell us more about a noun. Adjectives are **describing** words.

> the **green** grass   a **tall** man
>
> a **quiet** mouse   the **noisy** children

Comparative adjectives are used to compare two nouns.
- The dog is **bigger** than the cat.
- The green bus is **quicker** than the red one.

Superlative adjectives compare **more** than two nouns.
- Baby Bear's porridge was hot. Mummy Bear's porridge was hotter, but Daddy Bear's porridge was the **hottest.**
- My football team is the **greatest**.
- My car is fast. My dad's car is faster, but my brother's car is the **fastest**.

Practice activities

1. Look at the picture and write **three** adjectives to describe each one:

a)

_____

b)

_____

c)

_____

d)

_____

e)

_____

2. Make the adjectives in brackets into **comparative** adjectives.

a) My teacher is (kind) _____ than the others.

b) The playground is (large) _____ than my garden.

c) Our new baby is (noisy) _____ than me.

d) Monday was (hot) _____ than Tuesday.

e) The DVD I watched was (funny) _____ than the TV programme.

3. Write the correct adjective in the table below.

Adjective	Comparative	Superlative
hot	hotter	hottest
	prettier	
		tallest

4. **Underline** the **comparative** adjective and put a **circle** around the **superlative** adjective in each sentence.

a) In my class, Sophie is taller than James, but Lucy is the tallest.

b) The big swimming pool is colder than the small one, but the outside pool is the coldest.

c) My music is louder than my sister's, although my brother's music is the loudest.

d) After the games, the cricketer was dirty, the footballer was dirtier, but the rugby player was the dirtiest of all.

e) The red car was faster than the blue car, but the silver car was the fastest and won the race.

f) The tallest sunflower was 50cm longer than mine.

5. Look at the adjectives below. Write another adjective next to each one that has the same meaning.

big		nice	
hot		little	

Adjectives 2

Key to grammar

Whether writing or speaking, **adjectives** can make our sentences more interesting because they add detail and description. For example:

I am going to make sandcastles on the beach.

I am going to make **tall, golden** sandcastles on the **hot**, **sandy** beach.

Practice activities

1. Look at the words below. Circle the adjectives.

   green light   **old clothes**   **dirty bus**

   delicious cakes   **clever boy**   **soggy paper**

2. Underline the adjectives in the paragraph below.

   Yesterday, we went to the fair. It was amazing! There were bright, flashing lights and there was very loud music. I liked the big rides the best. The scariest ride was the ghost train, so I went on that with my dad. At the end of the day, we shared some warm, sticky doughnuts and bought some pink, fluffy candyfloss to take home.

Answers

Pages 4–5
1. a) b f k o r w y z
   b) h l
   c) v w x y
2. aeroplane, bus, car, train
3. a) cricket, football, swimming, tennis
   b) cheese, egg, ham, jam, tuna
   c) jacket, shoes, shorts, skirt, trousers, vest

Pages 6–7
1. a) question b) statement c) question
   d) statement
2. a) The car was red.
   b) Have you started reading your book?
   c) Be quiet!
   d) I like eating toast with jam on top.
3. a) question b) statement c) command
   d) statement e) question f) command
   g) command h) statement i) question
   j) statement

Pages 8–9
1. a) swim b) drive c) read/sit d) paint
2. a) Mrs Jones cooks tasty meals.
   b) Cinderella dances with Prince Charming at the ball.
   c) The shop sells lots of clothes.
   d) My brother listens to music on the computer.
3. eat, sleep, stretch, climb, jump, drink, pounce
4. a)–d) Accept any appropriate verbs,
   e.g.: a) run, eat, walk b) swim, move, glide c) hop, eat, jump d) gallop, jump, neigh

Pages 10–11
1. a) book b) train c) house d) tiger
2. a) bird b) airport c) teeth d) girl
3. a) table, cloth
   b) shops, bread, milk
   c) car, bucket, water, sponges
   d) boys, cricket, park, school
   e) mum, bedrooms, toys, floor
   f) ice cream
4. a) monkey b) beach, shells
   c) school, bag d) teacher, sweets
5. **Accept any grammatically correct sentence that includes two common nouns, e.g.:** The **parrot** copied what the **man** said.

Pages 12–13
1. a) The cows were in the field.
   b) The excited astronauts were trying on their new spacesuits.
   c) We are going to the library to listen to stories.
   d) The cats and dogs were making lots of noise because they were frightened of the loud fireworks.
   e) We have sandwiches, crisps, apples and sweets in our picnic today.
   f) There were lots of people waiting at the platform for the next two trains this morning.
2. a) women b) children c) teeth d) feet
3. a) teacher b) friends/teachers
   c) dogs, tails d) geese

Pages 14–15
1. Mrs Smith, April, Manchester, Max
2. a) January b) Sara c) Cardiff
3. a) flock b) swarm c) herd d) brood

Pages 16–17
1. verb
2. a) My friend's cat likes jumping.
   b) We ate dinner in the kitchen.
   c) I drank a cup of warm tea.
   d) Alex ran along the beach.
   e) Kara's pink bedroom was messy.
   f) He walked down the path.
   g) We can't go shopping in the heavy rain.
3. a) upside down
   b) of dirty plates
   c) small and quiet
   d) deep and cold
   e) at the park
   f) after lunch
4. a)–b) **Accept any suitable and grammatically correct ending to the sentences.**

Pages 18–19
1. a) because he was late
   b) As her dinner was ready
   c) even though she had cried
2. a) When the teacher came into the room, we stopped talking.
   b) We went to the park because the sun was shining.

1

Answers

c) I spent my pocket money, but <u>my grandad</u> <u>gave me some extra money</u>.

d) Although they are very noisy, <u>the drums</u> <u>are my favourite instrument</u>.

3. **a) Any suitable and grammatically correct complex sentence, e.g.:** The Oak tree, which is the largest in Sherwood Forest, is where Robin Hood once lived.

b) Any suitable and grammatically correct complex sentence, e.g.: The birthday cake, which had five candles on, was for my sister's party.

Pages 20–21

1. he, them, she, it, I, us

2. **a)** Charlie was tired, so <u>he</u> went upstairs to bed.

b) A spider crawled up the chair. <u>It</u> was large and black.

c) Rebecca played with some toys while <u>she</u> was on holiday.

d) Bethan doesn't eat many sweets because <u>she</u> knows <u>they</u> are bad for the teeth.

e) The builder came, but <u>we</u> were out.

f) "The ball is not <u>yours</u>. <u>It</u> is <u>mine</u>!" <u>he</u> shouted.

3. An old man on the point of death called his sons to give them some advice. He told them to bring in a bundle of sticks, and said to the eldest son:

"Break it."

The son really strained but was unable to break the bundle. The other sons tried too, but none of **them** could do it.

"Untie the bundle," said the father, "and each of **you** take a stick."

When **they** each had a stick, he said to them:

"Now, break them," and each stick broke easily. Their father then asked: "You see what **I** mean?"

4. Dexter read a long book even though **he** found **it** difficult.

Pages 22–23

1. **a)** Toby <u>shouted</u> at his brother.

b) The monkey <u>grabbed</u> a large bunch of bananas.

c) The children <u>will</u> <u>eat</u> their dinner in the hall.

d) We <u>are</u> <u>riding</u> our bikes to the park.

e) Emma and Tina <u>danced</u> at the disco last night.

f) I drink water because it <u>keeps</u> me healthy.

g) Charlotte <u>cried</u> when she <u>fell</u> off her scooter.

2.

Verb	Present	Past	Future
laugh	she laughs	she laughed	she will laugh
walk	**you walk**	you walked	you will walk
play	he plays	**he played**	**he will play**
talk	**we talk**	we talked	**we will talk**
skip	they skip	**they skipped**	they will skip

3. **a)** I worked hard at school.

b) I tidied my bedroom.

c) We jumped in muddy puddles.

d) I played with my toys.

4. **a)** has **b)** opened **c)** have

Pages 24–25

1. **a)** The sports day will <u>start</u> at four o'clock.

b) The girls will <u>play</u> football tomorrow.

c) Next week, I shall <u>walk</u> to school.

d) Tomorrow, I will <u>run</u> to school.

2.

Present tense	Future tense
I eat.	I will eat.
We cook.	**We will cook.**
They sit.	**They will sit.**

3. **a)** They will swim.

b) They will surf.

c) They will dance.

d) They will sleep.

4. **a)** play **b)** eat **c)** learn **d)** take **e)** juggle **f)** dive

Pages 26–27

1. **a)** break – broke **b)** know – knew **c)** go – went **d)** ride – rode **e)** do – did **f)** take – took **g)** swim – swam **h)** hear – heard

Answers

2. **a)** flew **b)** had **c)** sold
d) grew **e)** stood **f)** sat

3.

Present tense	Past tense
think	thought
grow	grew
find	**found**
make	**made**
say	said
blow	blew

4. **Accept any correct sentence.**

5. play; cook

Pages 28–29

1. **a)** were **b)** was **c)** was
d) were **e)** were **f)** was

2. Once upon a time, there <u>was</u> a lion lying by a tree. A little mouse <u>was</u> running up and down the lion's back, and he <u>was</u> beginning to make the lion angry. The lion turned its large head and opened its mouth widely. With its piercing eyes glaring, the lion <u>was</u> about to swallow the little mouse in one big gulp.
Just then the little mouse squeaked, "Please don't eat me! One day you might need me to help you."
The lion laughed but let the little mouse go free. He <u>was</u> sure he would never need help from such a small, pathetic creature. Then, one day, three men <u>were</u> walking through the forest holding nets. The men <u>were</u> trying to catch the lion and swiftly threw a net over the lion's strong body. The lion roared and struggled, but there <u>was</u> nothing he could do. He could not escape.
Just then the little mouse returned to help the lion. He began, very slowly, to gnaw and chew through the net with his sharp teeth. Eventually, the mouse made a hole that <u>was</u> wide enough for the lion to escape.

3. **a)** Were **b)** Was **c)** Were **d)** Was

Pages 30–31

1. **a)** did **b)** done **c)** did **d)** did
2. **a)** did **b)** done **c)** done
d) Did **e)** done **f)** did

3. **a)** I have done nothing wrong!
b) We did a handstand together.
c) They did very well in their swimming lesson.

4. **a)–b)** Accept any correct sentences using **did** and **done**.

Pages 32–33

1. **a)** The dirty, old dog ran <u>into</u> the house.
b) Jessica sat <u>next to</u> her friend.
c) Sam jumped <u>in</u> muddy puddles.
d) The football team ran <u>around</u> the pitch.
e) The ant is <u>under</u> the rock.

2. under, after, over, on, below

3. **a)** The book is on the table.
b) The fox is in / under a box.
c) The cat is under / beneath the table.
d) The sun is behind the cloud.
(**a/an** instead of **the** also correct)

4. **a)** into **b)** next to **c)** behind **d)** over

Pages 34–35

1. **a)–e)** **Accept any suitable adjectives,**
e.g.: a) cute, furry, small **b)** big, grey, heavy **c)** long, yellow, bright **d)** sandy, hot, warm **e)** fiery, hot, yellow

2. **a)** kinder **b)** larger **c)** noisier
d) hotter **e)** funnier

3.

Adjective	Comparative	Superlative
hot	hotter	hottest
pretty	prettier	**prettiest**
tall	**taller**	tallest

4. **a)** taller, (tallest) **b)** colder, (coldest)
c) louder, (loudest) **d)** dirtier, (dirtiest)
e) faster, (fastest) **f)** longer, (tallest)

5. **a)–d)** **Any adjectives that are synonyms, e.g.**

big	large
hot	warm

nice	kind
little	small

Pages 36–37

1. green, old, dirty, delicious, clever, soggy

2. Yesterday, we went to the fair. It was <u>amazing</u>! There were <u>bright</u>, <u>flashing</u> lights and there was very <u>loud</u> music. I liked the <u>big</u> rides the best. The <u>scariest</u> ride was the ghost train, so I went on that with my dad. At the end of the day, we shared some

Answers

warm, sticky doughnuts and bought some pink, fluffy candyfloss to take home.

3. **Accept any suitable adjectives.**

4. **a)–b) Accept any suitable adjectives relating to the nouns.**

5. **Accept any appropriate adjectives. For example:** Today was brilliant as it was our school's sports day! The **green** field was covered in **bouncy** balls, bats, **tangled** skipping ropes, **soft** bean bags and many more **fun** games. Our class was split into four teams. I was in the **red** team! Lots of **excited** mums and dads were sitting on **small** chairs, waiting for us to start our activities and races. When the **loud** whistle blew, we were off. Ready, steady, go!

Pages 38–39

1. **a)** slowly **b)** fiercely **c)** loudly
   d) patiently **e)** carefully, gently **f)** angrily

2. **Any suitable adverbs, e.g.**

talk	run	drink	dance
quietly	quickly	noisily	beautifully
loudly	smoothly	thirstily	awkwardly

3. At my birthday party, there was a clever magician who waved his wand gently over a special box. He shouted the magic words loudly three times, then asked for a helper from the audience. Excitedly, I put up my hand, and before I could change my mind, the magician had chosen me. I went bravely to the front of the stage and helped him mysteriously produce a floppy-eared, soft, white rabbit. Everyone loved the trick and clapped enthusiastically at the end.

4. **a)** Before **b)** sometimes **c)** outside
   d) Yesterday

5. **a)** Soon **b)** loudly **c)** busily **d)** Perhaps

Pages 40–41

1. **a)** On Friday, I walked for half an hour.
   b) I met my friends outside school.
   c) I usually go and visit my grandma on a Wednesday.
   d) Dan ate some chocolate after his tea.
   e) Kosha practised playing the violin every day.

2. **a)** how often **b)** where **c)** when
   d) where and when **e)** where

3. **a)** Quickly, the horse galloped down the track.
   b) Swiftly, the bird darted through the sky.
   c) Gently, the little girl stroked the purring cat.
   d) Gracefully, the gymnast flew through the air.

4. **Accept any sentence that makes sense and starts with a fronted adverbial, e.g.:** Eagerly, the geese pecked at the bread.

Pages 42–43

1. **a)** The girl put on a jumper
   b) I need a paint brush.
   c) I had an egg for breakfast.

2. Words starting with a consonant sound under **a**; words starting with a vowel sound under **an**.

3. **a)** a trumpet **b)** an elephant
   c) an umbrella **d)** a game
   e) a holiday **f)** an insect

4. **a)** I need to wear **a/the** sunhat when **the** sun is shining.
   b) I saw **an/the** ant crawling along **the** leaves.
   c) When I go to **the** shops, I need to buy **a** loaf of bread.
   d) **The/A** teacher read **a/the** story in assembly this morning.
   e) Alicia had **a** tummy ache after eating too many cakes.

5. **a)** Paige likes reading **the/a** book about dinosaurs.
   b) I will be back in **an** hour.
   c) **The** animals were waiting to see the vet.

Pages 44–45

1. **a)** I like oranges, but my sister prefers apples.
   b) I am feeling cold and I have a headache.
   c) My dad said I could have a new bike if I keep my bedroom tidy.
   d) We have a different teacher today because Mrs Power is ill.

2. **a)** unless **b)** because **c)** so **d)** but **e)** and

3. **Accept any sentences using the given conjunctions that make sense, e.g.:**
   a) I am hungry because I didn't eat any dinner.

b) I have lots of homework tonight so I can't see my friends.

c) Would you like chicken or fish for tea?

d) We can play outside unless it rains heavily.

e) The children like to go swimming when the weather is hot.

Pages 46–47

1. **a)** I need to be at school <u>before</u> nine o'clock.

   b) When I make a cake, I read the recipe. <u>Next</u>, I find the ingredients I need.

   c) "You can go and play outside <u>as soon as</u> it has stopped raining," my mum said.

   d) Mr Bull helped our class learn some new songs, <u>then</u> he helped another class.

   e) We have been waiting for the bus to arrive <u>since</u> nine o'clock.

   f) My birthday is in June, <u>then</u> it will be Amy's in July.

   g) <u>When</u> the plane <u>finally</u> arrived in Spain, I was feeling very excited.

2. **a)** First **b)** Next **c)** then **d)** as soon as **e)** When **f)** Meanwhile **g)** Finally

3. **Accept any sentences that make sense and use the time connectives, e.g.:**

   a) Next I will brush my teeth.

   b) I will tidy my bedroom then play a game.

   c) As soon as it is 8pm, I will go to bed.

Pages 48–49

1. Oh, no! – exclamation
   Where are you going? – question
   The sea was very cold. – statement
   (**1 mark** for all three correct)

2. put (**1 mark**)

3.

Present tense	Past tense
play	**played**
swim	swam
laugh	laughed
build	**built**
run	**ran**
cry	cried
fall	**fell**

(**2 marks** for all correct; **1 mark** for 3–6 correct)

4. The <u>smartest</u> dog won first prize in the dog show last night. (**1 mark**)

5. Cautiously and carefully, Sam lifted the cakes out of the oven. (**1 mark**)

6. bike, cousin, scooter (**1 mark** for all 3 correct)

7. she (**1 mark**)

8. because (**1 mark**)

9. Everyone is going to the cinema tonight. (**1 mark**)

10. When they were young, <u>the children loved going camping</u>. (**1 mark**)

11. I have done all my homework. (**1 mark**)

Pages 50–51

1. **a)** I am going to go to After School Club today.

   b) The farmer has lots of animals in his field.

   c) We are going to the seaside tomorrow. I am looking forward to it.

   d) "Help! Help!' they shouted. The children were stuck inside the shed. They couldn't get out.

2. **Accept any suitable sentences about each picture that correctly use a full stop, e.g.:**

   a) My favourite toy is my teddy bear called Big Ted.

   b) I love playing on the swings with my brother.

3. Dear Daddy Bear, Mummy Bear and Baby Bear,

   I am so sorry that I broke into your house. I was very hungry and could see your lovely bowls of porridge cooling on the table. Baby Bear, your porridge was delicious. It tasted just right.

   After eating all the porridge, I decided to have a rest. I didn't mean to break the chair in your living room. I didn't know what to do, so I went upstairs and hid. I loved Baby Bear's bed. It was so comfy! I must have fallen asleep before you came back. You seemed very cross with me so I ran out of your cottage and hid further down the path. I didn't want to get into trouble.

   I hope one day you will forgive me and we can be friends.

   Lots of love, Goldilocks xxx

Answers

4. Dear Goldilocks,

   Thank you for your letter. We accept your apology and hope we can now be friends. Would you like to come round to our cottage again sometime? Maybe we could cook you some tea. Baby Bear would love to play with you in the garden. Please let us know if you would like that too.

   Lots of love, The Three Bears xxx

Pages 52–53

1. Once upon a time, there was a little old lady and a little old man. One day, they decided to bake a gingerbread man, so they made him carefully and then put him in the oven to cook.

   When the Gingerbread Man was ready, the little old lady opened the oven door, but, … oh, no! The Gingerbread Man ran away! Before the little old man and the little old lady had blinked, the Gingerbread Man had run out of the house and was halfway up the road.

   "Run, run as fast as you can! You can't catch me. I'm the Gingerbread Man!"

   "Help!" cried the little old lady to a nearby farmer.

   "Quick, run!" shouted the farmer, "We can catch him!"

   But the Gingerbread Man continued to run, still singing. "Run, run as fast as you can! You can't catch me. I'm the Gingerbread Man!"

2. **Accept any suitable sentences that use an exclamation mark and are grammatically correct, e.g.:**
   a) Ouch! I have hurt my finger!
   b) Stop it! Please don't argue anymore!
   c) Don't touch! The iron is hot!
   d) Quick, run! We can win the race!
   e) Help! Help! I'm stuck in the lift!

3. Go away! – an order
   Ouch! – pain
   Wow! – surprise

Pages 54–55

1. a) Please can someone help me?
   b) Would you like to go to the playground today?
   c) Where is the train station?

2. a) I am going outside to play in the snow.
   b) Are you ready for the race tomorrow?
   c) Which colour do you prefer?
   d) Where are my shoes? I can't find them anywhere.
   e) The children were excited about the school disco.

3. **Accept any suitable questions that are grammatically correct and use the relevant question word, e.g.:**
   a) Where is the bus going?
   b) When would you use a tour bus?
   c) How many levels does the bus have?
   d) What time of day is shown in the picture?
   e) Which is the tallest building?
   f) Have you ever been to London?

Pages 56–57

1. a) december, paul, france, david
   b) i) December ii) Paul iii) France iv) David

2. Today will be a warm, dry day. It will start cloudy in most areas of England and Wales, but by lunchtime the sun will be shining! Devon and Cornwall will see the highest temperatures, whereas Lincolnshire and Yorkshire will be the coolest.
   Tonight will remain warm and slightly humid, and tomorrow and Thursday we may see some heavy thunderstorms.

3. a) On a Monday evening, Leah and Kate go to choir practice.
   b) My birthday is in March, but my sister's birthday is in August.
   c) Mr Thomson's pupils were being very noisy because they were practising a play.
   d) Pebbles was a shy cat who didn't like Mrs Stone, the vet.
   e) Our favourite sport is football. We play it every Saturday at the park.

Pages 58–59

1. a) I am wearing trousers, a T-shirt, socks and shoes.
   b) My favourite colours are red, blue, green, yellow and silver.
   c) My mum can play the piano, the flute and the clarinet.
   d) I like playing on the swings, slide and roundabout.

Answers

e) My favourite subjects at school are English, music, science and PE.

f) My cousins are called Chloe, Jules, Safa and Joe.

g) On holiday I went to the beach, the swimming pool, the disco and the museum.

2. a) The fish is yellow, blue, green and gold.

b) My sandwich has ham, cheese, butter and pickle in it.

3. a) I would like some bread, milk, jam, eggs and sugar.

b) I need apples, oranges, bananas, strawberries and pears.

c) I must remember to buy some peas, carrots, broccoli, celery and tomatoes.

Pages 60–61

1. a) "Sweep the floors and iron our clothes, Cinderella!" shouted the Ugly Sisters.

b) "Hurry up with the washing, Cinderella!"

c) Cinderella whispered to herself, "I would love to wear a pretty dress."

2. a) "How long is it until dinner is ready?" Sam asked.

b) "What time do you usually go to bed?"

c) "Please can I go to the park, Mum?" Rachel asked.

d) "Oh no!" sighed Dad.

e) "Where would you like to go on holiday?" Mum and Dad asked.

f) The man next door shouted, "Keep the noise down, please!"

g) The teacher shouted, "Sit down everyone!"

h) "Have you eaten all your dinner today?" Mum asked.

3. a) "What time does your party start?" Olivia asked.

b) "Can I have a drink of water, please?" Radi asked his teacher.

c) "Go and put your shoes on!" Mum shouted.

Pages 62–63

1. a) "I love going to school," Ben said.

b) "The train is delayed, so I'm going to be home late," Dad grumbled.

c) "Can you tell me where the nearest shop is, please?"

d) "Ouch!" Mrs Baker shouted. "I've hurt my toe!"

2. a) "What time are you leaving?" I asked my friends.

b) "We will be going at about two o'clock," they replied.

c) "Can I come too?" I asked.

d) "Of course you can."

3. a) "Hurry up! You'll be late!" Mum yelled up the stairs.
    "I'm coming!" I replied.

b) "Hello. How can I help you?" the doctor asked.
    "I have a nasty cough and a very sore throat," I replied.

c) "What would you like in your lunch box tomorrow?" Dad asked.
    "Please can I have ham sandwiches with tomatoes and crisps?" I answered.
    "Of course you can."

d) "Has everyone got a piece of paper?" Mr Evans asked.
    "I haven't," I said.
    "Don't worry! I will get you one," he replied.

Pages 64–65

1. Little Red Riding Hood skipped out of her house and ran through the forest to her grandma's house. While she was running, she saw some beautiful flowers and stopped to pick some.

    When she arrived at her grandma's house, she went straight into the bedroom, but something was wrong. Little Red Riding Hood thought her grandma looked very strange today.

2. **Accept any three clear and grammatically correct paragraphs.**

Pages 66–67

1. Ouch!
    Where are you?
    I like drinking milk.
    (*1 mark* for all three correct)

2. When we went to the farm, I saw cows, hens, sheep, geese and ducks. (*1 mark* for all three correct)

Answers

3. **a)** Lisa won first prize in a colouring competition. She was very happy. *(1 mark for the two capital letters, 1 mark for the two full stops)*

   b) I love cooking with my mum. When I am older, I would like to be a chef. *(1 mark for the four capital letters, 1 mark for the two full stops)*

4. Is it Wednesday today? *(1 mark)*

5. **Accept any question that is grammatically correct and uses a question mark. (1 mark)**

6. **Accept any sentence that is grammatically correct and uses an exclamation mark. (1 mark)**

7. Inverted commas *(1 mark)*

8. **a)** Darcey, Elizabeth, Tom, France. *(1 mark)*
   b) It is a proper noun. *(1 mark)*

9. "Is anyone there?" shouted Mia. *(1 mark)*

10. "Can I go and play at Toby's house, please?" I asked Mum.
    Mum replied, "Of course you can."
    (1 mark for each correct sentence)

11. When the writing changes time, action, event, place or person. *(2 marks for any two from this list)*

Pages 68–71

1. David hit the ball so hard it smashed a window. *(1 mark)*

2. The birds swooped and darted through the sky. *(1 mark)*

3. Ouch, I've hurt my finger! – Exclamation
   I need a plaster. – Statement
   My finger is bleeding. – Statement
   (1 mark for all three correct)

4. **Any suitable adjective, e.g.:** rough, blue, fierce, etc. *(1 mark)*

5.

singular	plural
car	**cars**
mouse	mice
knife	**knives**

(1 mark for all 3 correct)

6. **a) an** elephant **b) a** frog
   (1 mark for both correct)

7. **a)** At the weekend I go swimming, play football, see friends and watch TV.
   (1 mark)
   b) September, April, June and November all have thirty days.
   (1 mark)

8. because *(1 mark)*

9. **a)** The children **were** dancing./The **child** was dancing. *(1 mark)*
   b) Mike **was** laughing. *(1 mark)*

10. I **will ask** for more. *(1 mark)*

11. a, e, i *(1 mark)*

12. **Accept any two clear and grammatically correct questions, e.g.:**
    a) How long did it take to write your book?
    (1 mark)
    b) Who is your favourite character in the story? *(1 mark)*

13. library, books *(1 mark for both correct answers)*

14. gracefully *(1 mark)*

15. **Any suitable adverb, e.g.** clumsily, awkwardly, nicely, etc. *(1 mark)*

16. Jake and **I** watched his dad wash the car.
    (1 mark)
    "You splashed **me**!" I shouted. *(1 mark)*

17. she *(1 mark)*

18. in *(1 mark)*

19. "I like your new glasses," Jamie said. "Thank you!" replied Michelle.
    (1 mark for both correct)

20. "You shouldn't feed the animals," the zookeeper said. *(1 mark)*

21. Charlie cycled to school this morning **although** usually he walks. *(1 mark)*

ISBN 9781844198689

Text, design and illustration © Letts Educational, an imprint of HarperCollins*Publishers* Ltd

3. Now read the same paragraph and fill in the gaps with some **new** adjectives.

Yesterday, we went to the _____ fair. It was

_____. There were _____, flashing lights and

there was very _____ music. I liked the _____

rides the best. The scariest ride was the ghost train, so I went on that with

my _____ dad. At the end of the _____ day,

we shared some warm, _____ doughnuts and bought some

_____, _____ candyfloss to take home.

4. Rewrite these sentences using adjectives to make your writing more exciting.

a) The teacher stood in the playground.

_____

_____

b) The firefighter put out the fire.

_____

_____

5. Fill in the blanks with adjectives of your choice.

Today was brilliant as it was our school's sports day! The _____

field was covered in _____ balls, bats, _____

skipping ropes, _____ bean bags and many more

_____ games. Our class was split into four teams. I was in the

_____ team! Lots of _____ mums and dads were

sitting on _____ chairs, waiting for us to start our activities

and races. When the _____ whistle blew, we were off. Ready,

steady, go!

Adverbs 1

Adverbs describe a verb. Adverbs tell us **how**, **when** or **where** something happens or is done.

> James **quickly** ate his tea.

Adverbs often end with the suffix **ly**. Adverbs that don't end in **ly** include many **when** or **where** adverbs. For example:
- He **sometimes** read. (*when*)
- He read **inside**. (*where*)

Practice activities

1. Look at the sentences below. Circle the adverb(s) in each one.

   a) The artist painted the flower slowly.

   b) The dragon roared fiercely and blew fire out of his nose.

   c) The children shouted loudly in the playground.

   d) Patiently, the audience waited for the show to begin.

   e) Carefully and gently, the nurse bandaged his leg.

   f) The wasp flew angrily around our food.

2. Complete the table below with adverbs that can be used to describe each verb.

talk	run	drink	dance

3. Read the passage below. Underline all the adverbs that show **how** the verb is done.

At my birthday party, there was a clever magician who waved his wand gently over a special box. He shouted the magic words loudly three times, then asked for a helper from the audience. Excitedly, I put up my hand, and before I could change my mind, the magician had chosen me. I went bravely to the front of the stage and helped him mysteriously produce a floppy-eared, soft, white rabbit. Everyone loved the trick and clapped enthusiastically at the end.

4. Choose one of the adverbs from the box below to add to each sentence.

sometimes	Before	Yesterday	outside

a) _____ they started, the players warmed up.

b) I _____ fall out with my brother.

c) I like playing _____ on the trampoline.

d) _____ it was my birthday.

5. Put a circle around the adverb that fits best in each sentence.

a) **Soon / Never** it will be summer.

b) The children giggled **loudly / carefully**.

c) The teacher **busily / warmly** marked the children's work.

d) **Perhaps / Never** you could come to my house for tea?

Adverbs 2

An **adverbial phrase** is a group of words that act like an adverb, giving more information about **how**, **when**, **where** or **why** something is done. For example:

- Clara jumped **into the water.** (tells us **where**)
- We have been **at this school for five years**. (tells us **where** and **when**)

Fronted adverbials are when an adverb or adverbial phrase has been moved to the **beginning** of a sentence. They are used to create effect and make writing more interesting. A comma is used after a fronted adverbial.

Carefully, the cat walked along the roof.

In 1948, they were married.

1. Read the sentences below and underline the adverbial phrases.

   a) On Friday, I walked for half an hour.

   b) I met my friends outside school.

   c) I usually go and visit my grandma on a Wednesday.

   d) Dan ate some chocolate after his tea.

   e) Kosha practised playing the violin every day.

2. Read the sentences below and write whether the adverbial phrases are showing **where**, **when** or **how often** something happens. Some sentences may have more than one answer.

a) I have a shower every day. _____

b) My brother hid his homework under his bed. _____

c) The dog barked when he went for a walk. _____

d) I go to the library on a Wednesday afternoon. _____

e) Our English lesson was in the hall. _____

3. Rewrite these sentences putting the adverb at the **front** of the sentence.

a) The horse galloped quickly down the track.

_____

b) The bird darted swiftly through the sky.

_____

c) The little girl stroked the purring cat gently.

_____

d) The gymnast flew gracefully through the air.

_____

4. Write a fronted adverbial phrase of your own.

_____

Determiners

A **determiner** stands before a noun or a word that describes the noun (an adjective). The most common determiners are **the**, **a** and **an**.

Before a word beginning with a consonant sound we use **a**, but before a word beginning with a vowel sound we use **an** (sometimes **h** at the start of a word can be silent, so we use **an** rather than **a**).

a spider   **a** hotel   **an** octopus   **an** hour

Practice activities

1. Underline the determiners in each sentence.

   a) The girl put on a jumper.

   b) I need a paint brush.

   c) I had an egg for breakfast.

2. Fill the table below with words that would follow **a** or **an**. Two have been added to the table already, as examples.

a	an
boy	egg

3. Read the words below and decide whether to use **a** or **an**.

a) _____ trumpet

b) _____ elephant

c) _____ umbrella

d) _____ game

e) _____ holiday

f) _____ insect

4. Choose **a**, **an** or **the** to fill in the gaps in the sentences below.

a) I need to wear _____ sunhat when _____ sun is shining.

b) I saw _____ ant crawling along _____ leaves.

c) When I go to _____ shops, I need to buy _____ loaf of bread.

d) _____ teacher read _____ story in assembly this morning.

e) Alicia had _____ tummy ache after eating too many cakes.

5. Rewrite these sentences correctly, replacing **a**, **an** or **the** with the correct word.

a) Paige likes reading an book about dinosaurs.

_____

b) I will be back in a hour.

_____

c) A animals were waiting to see the vet.

_____

Conjunctions

Key to grammar

Conjunctions are connecting words. They link words, phrases, clauses or sentences.

Some common conjunctions are:

and	but	so	if
because		or	when
yet	although	unless	for

You must take your shoes off **so** you don't get dirt on the carpet.

We need to wash our hands **because** it is nearly dinner time.

Although Missy was only small, she had a very loud bark!

Practice activities

1. Underline the conjunctions in the sentences.

   a) I like oranges, but my sister prefers apples.

   b) I am feeling cold and I have a headache.

   c) My dad said I could have a new bike if I keep my bedroom tidy.

   d) We have a different teacher today because Mrs Power is ill.

2. Choose the correct conjunction from the box below to add to the sentences.

because	and	so	but	unless

a) _____ I feel better tomorrow, I will need to see a doctor.

b) The baby cried _____ he was hungry.

c) It is raining, _____ I will need to put on my coat.

d) I like eating chocolate, _____ Natasha prefers ice cream!

e) We are going to the cinema _____ we are going to buy some popcorn.

3. Write sentences using the conjunctions in brackets.

a) (**because**) _____

_____

b) (**so**) _____

_____

c) (**or**) _____

_____

d) (**unless**) _____

_____

e) (**when**) _____

_____

Time connectives

Key to grammar

Time connectives are used to show the passing of time. They link words and sentences together to show the order in which events happen or have happened.

Here are some examples:

by the time	since	when	finally
as soon as		before	next	then
after	later	firstly	meanwhile	eventually

Practice activities

1. Underline the time connectives in the sentences.

   a) I need to be at school before nine o'clock.

   b) When I make a cake, I read the recipe. Next, I find the ingredients I need.

   c) "You can go outside to play as soon as it has stopped raining," my mum said.

   d) Mr Bull helped our class learn some new songs, then he helped another class.

   e) We have been waiting for the bus to arrive since nine o'clock.

   f) My birthday is in June, then it will be Amy's in July.

   g) When the plane finally arrived in Spain, I was feeling very excited.

2. Look at the instructions below for baking a cake. Choose a time connective from the box and write it in the correct place.

as soon as	First	Finally
Meanwhile	then	Next	When

a) _____, weigh the ingredients.

b) _____, put the sugar and butter in a bowl and mix well.

c) Add two eggs and stir carefully, _____ add sieved flour.

d) Fold the flour into the mixture and _____ the flour is well mixed, pour the mixture into the cake tin.

e) _____ the mixture is in the cake tin, put it into the oven for forty minutes.

f) _____, tidy the kitchen and wash the bowls.

g) _____, take the cake out of the oven and let it cool.

3. Write sentences using the connectives in brackets.

a) (**next**) _____

_____

b) (**then**) _____

_____

c) (**as soon as**) _____

_____

Test your grammar

These questions will help you to practise the grammar skills you have learned in this book. They will also help you prepare for the grammar and punctuation test that you will take in Year 6 at the end of Key Stage 2.

Make sure you read each question carefully and do what it asks. The questions slowly get harder to help you progress steadily.

1. Draw a line to match the words to the correct sentence structure.

Oh no!	question
Where are you going?	statement
The sea was very cold.	exclamation

1 mark

2. Circle the **verb** in this sentence.

    Mum put on her shoes quickly.

1 mark

3. Look at the table below. Fill in the gaps.

Present tense	Past tense
play	
	swam
	laughed
build	
run	
	cried
fall	

2 marks

4. Underline the **superlative adjective** in this sentence

  The smartest dog won first prize in the dog show last night.   *1 mark*

5. Which sentence contains **two adverbs**?

                                                                    Tick **one**

  Slowly the car pulled away down the winding driveway.   ☐

  Emily danced gracefully at the party.   ☐

  Cautiously and carefully, Sam lifted the cakes out of the oven.   ☐

  The dog ate the food hungrily and then looked for more.   ☐

                                                                    1 mark

6. Read the sentence below and circle all the **nouns**.

  I rode on my bike while my cousin rode his scooter.   *1 mark*

7. Read the sentence below. Choose the most suitable **pronoun** to fill the gap.

  Jessica went to the theatre and _____ watched a play.

  she   **her**   **it**   **me**   *1 mark*

8. Circle the **conjunction** in the sentence below.

  Lucy was feeling excited because it was her birthday tomorrow.   *1 mark*

9. In which sentence do the **subject** and **verb** agree?

                                                      Tick **one**

  Most of my friends likes drinking lemonade.   ☐

  Girls is reading books in the library.   ☐

  Everyone is going to the cinema tonight.   ☐

  The dog live in the kennels.   ☐

  The man swim in the sea.   ☐

                                                      1 mark

10. Underline the **main clause** in this sentence.

  When they were young, the children loved going camping.   *1 mark*

11. Write this sentence in the **present perfect tense**.

  I did all my homework.   *1 mark*

Full stops

Key to punctuation

Most sentences end with a **full stop**.

Tom went into the library to borrow a book**.**

This morning, I decided to bake a cake**.** I had to go to the shops to buy the ingredients**.**

Practice activities

1. Read the sentences below and put full stops in the correct places.

    a) I am going to go to After School Club today

    b) The farmer has lots of animals in his field

    c) We are going to the seaside tomorrow I am looking forward to it

    d) "Help! Help!" they shouted The children were stuck inside the shed They couldn't get out

2. Look at the pictures and write **one sentence** about each one.
    Do not forget to use a full stop.

    a)

    _____

    _____

    b)

    _____

    _____

3. Goldilocks has forgotten to use full stops in her letter to the Three Bears. Read the letter then add the full stops in the correct places.

> *Dear Daddy Bear, Mummy Bear and Baby Bear,*
>
> *I am so sorry that I broke into your house I was very hungry and could see your lovely bowls of porridge cooling on the table Baby Bear, your porridge was delicious It tasted just right*
>
> *After eating all the porridge, I decided to have a rest I didn't mean to break the chair in your living room I didn't know what to do, so I went upstairs and hid I loved Baby Bear's bed It was so comfy! I must have fallen asleep before you came back You seemed very cross with me so I ran out of your cottage and hid further down the path I didn't want to get into trouble*
>
> *I hope one day you will forgive me and we can be friends*
>
> *Lots of love,*
>
> *Goldilocks xxx*

4. The Three Bears have replied to Goldilocks but they have put the full stops in the wrong places. Rewrite their letter below, putting the full stops in correctly.

> *Dear Goldilocks,*
>
> *Thank you. for your letter We accept your apology. and hope we can now be friends Would. you like to come round to our cottage. again sometime? Maybe we could. cook you some. tea. Baby Bear would love to play. with you in the garden Please let us know. if you would like that. too.*
>
> *Lots of love,*
>
> *The Three Bears xxx*

_____

_____

_____

_____

_____

Exclamation marks

An **exclamation mark** can be used at the end of a command to show it is urgent. For example:

- Go away**!**
- Quick, run**!**

An exclamation mark can also be used at the end of a sentence to show emotion, such as happiness, excitement, pain or anger. For example:

- How wonderful**!**
- That's a disgrace**!**

Practice activities

1. Read this story about the Gingerbread Man and add **nine** exclamation marks in the correct places.

   Once upon a time, there was a little old lady and a little old man. One day, they decided to bake a gingerbread man, so they made him carefully and then put him in the oven to cook.

   When the Gingerbread Man was ready, the little old lady opened the oven door, but, … oh, no The Gingerbread Man ran away Before the little old man and the little old lady had blinked, the Gingerbread Man had run out of the house and was halfway up the road.

   " Run, run as fast as you can You can't catch me. I'm the Gingerbread Man "

   " Help " cried the little old lady to a nearby farmer.

   " Quick, run " shouted the farmer, " We can catch him "

   But the Gingerbread Man continued to run, still singing. " Run, run as fast as you can You can't catch me. I'm the Gingerbread Man "

2. Look at the exclamations and write a sentence after each one. Do not forget to include an exclamation mark.

Example: Oh, no!

   Oh, no! My toast is burnt!

a) **Ouch!**

_____

b) **Stop it!**

_____

c) **Don't touch!**

_____

d) **Quick, run!**

_____

e) **Help!**

_____

3. Draw lines to match each exclamation with its correct description.

Ouch!		an order
Wow!		pain
Go away!		surprise

Question marks

Key to punctuation

A **question mark** is used at the end of a sentence when a question is being asked. A question mark is used instead of a full stop.

Are you ready to order**?**

Practice activities

1. Read the questions below. Put a question mark in the correct place.

   a) Please can someone help me

   b) Would you like to go to the playground today

   c) Where is the train station

2. Read the sentences below. Decide which ones are questions and which ones are statements and then put either a question mark or a full stop in the correct place.

   a) I am going outside to play in the snow

   b) Are you ready for the race tomorrow

   c) Which colour do you prefer

   d) Where are my shoes I can't find them anywhere

   e) The children were excited about the school disco

3. Look at the pictures of London.

Write questions about the pictures starting with the different question words below. Do not forget to end each question with a question mark.

Example: Could <u>we catch the bus?</u>

a) **Where** _____

b) **When** _____

c) **How** _____

d) **What** _____

e) **Which** _____

f) **Have** _____

Capital letters

Key to punctuation

A capital letter is used at the **start** of every sentence.

A **capital letter** is also always used at the start of a **proper noun** (the name of something or someone) and for the pronoun **I**.

Mary	December	Australia

Proper nouns and the pronoun **I** always start with a capital letter, even if they are in the middle of a sentence.

Practice activities

1. a) Look at the nouns below.

Put a circle around the ones that should start with a capital letter.

december   paul   shop

seaside   cat

france   david   garden

b) Write the nouns you have circled in part a), using a capital letter.

i) _____   ii) _____

iii) _____   iv) _____

2. Read the weather report below.

Put a circle around the letters that should be capital letters.

today will be a warm, dry day. it will start cloudy in most areas of england and wales, but by lunchtime the sun will be shining! devon and cornwall will see the highest temperatures, whereas lincolnshire and yorkshire will be the coolest.

tonight will remain warm and slightly humid, and tomorrow and thursday we may see some heavy thunderstorms.

3. Rewrite the sentences below using capital letters in the correct places.

a) on a monday evening, leah and kate go to choir practice.

_____

_____

b) my birthday is in march, but my sister's birthday is in august.

_____

_____

c) mr thomson's pupils were being very noisy because they were practising a play.

_____

_____

d) pebbles was a shy cat who didn't like mrs stone, the vet.

_____

_____

e) our favourite sport is football. we play it every saturday at the park.

_____

_____

Commas in a list

Commas are used to separate words in a list.

In my shopping basket there are eggs, milk and bread.

I like playing tennis, football, cricket and badminton.

The final word in a list is joined to the others with another word (usually **and**) instead of using a comma.

Practice activities

1. Put commas in the correct places in these sentences.

   a) I am wearing trousers a T-shirt socks and shoes.

   b) My favourite colours are red blue green yellow and silver.

   c) My mum can play the piano the flute and the clarinet.

   d) I like playing on the swings slide and roundabout.

   e) My favourite subjects at school are English music science and PE.

   f) My cousins are called Chloe Jules Safa and Joe.

   g) On holiday I went to the beach the swimming pool the disco and the museum.

2. Some of the commas in the sentences below are in the wrong place or are not needed. Rewrite the sentences placing commas where they are needed.

a) The fish, is, yellow, blue, green, and, gold.

_____

_____

b) My sandwich, has, ham, cheese, butter, and, pickle in it.

_____

_____

3. Use the shopping lists in the boxes to finish the sentences below.

a) bread	**b)** apples	**c)** peas
milk	oranges	carrots
jam	bananas	broccoli
eggs	strawberries	celery
sugar	pears	tomatoes

a) I would like some _____

_____

b) I need _____

_____

c) I must remember to buy some _____

_____

Direct speech 1

Key to punctuation

Direct speech is what a speaker actually says. When we write, we put **inverted commas** around direct speech. These are sometimes known as **speech marks**.

If the sentence begins with direct speech, we add a comma, exclamation mark or question mark just before the closing inverted commas and then usually let the reader know who said it.

> "I wish I could go to the ball,"
> Cinderella said.

If the sentence begins by telling us who is speaking, a comma should appear before the speech begins. When the direct speech finishes, it should normally end with a full stop, question mark or exclamation mark just before the closing inverted commas.

> The Fairy Godmother replied,
> "You shall go to the ball!"

Practice activities

1. Put inverted commas around what is being said below.

   a) Sweep the floors and iron our clothes, Cinderella! shouted the Ugly Sisters.

   b) Hurry up with the washing, Cinderella!

   c) Cinderella whispered to herself, I would love to wear a pretty dress.

2. Put inverted commas and punctuation in the correct places in the sentences below.

a) How long is it until dinner is ready   Sam asked

b) What time do you usually go to bed

c) Please can I go to the park, Mum   Rachel asked

d) Oh no   sighed Dad

e) Where would you like to go on holiday   Mum and Dad asked

f) The man next door shouted   Keep the noise down, please

g) The teacher shouted   Sit down everyone

h) Have you eaten all your dinner today   Mum asked

3. Rewrite these sentences adding inverted commas in the correct place.

a) What time does your party start? Olivia asked.

_____

_____

b) Can I have a drink of water, please? Radi asked his teacher.

_____

_____

c) Go and put your shoes on! Mum shouted.

_____

_____

Direct speech 2

In a conversation between two or more people, when a new person starts speaking, the speech is written on a **new line**.

"Please can I have some new rollerblades?" I asked my mum hopefully.

Mum replied, "You will have to wait until it is your birthday."

"But that is ages away!"

"You could save your pocket money," Mum suggested, "and buy some yourself."

Notice that all direct speech starts with a **capital letter**, except where the sentence of direct speech is broken by information about who is talking.

N.B. **inverted commas** are also called speech marks.

Practice activities

1. Put inverted commas around what is being said in these sentences.

    a) I love going to school, Ben said.

    b) The train is delayed, so I'm going to be home late, Dad grumbled.

    c) Can you tell me where the nearest shop is, please?

    d) Ouch! Mrs Baker shouted. I've hurt my toe!

2. Add inverted commas and the correct punctuation to these sentences.

a) What time are you leaving I asked my friends

b) We will be going at about two o'clock they replied

c) Can I come too I asked

d) Of course you can

3. Rewrite these conversations using inverted commas and the correct punctuation. Remember to start a new line for each new speaker.

a) Hurry up You'll be late Mum yelled up the stairs I'm coming I replied

_____

_____

b) Hello How can I help you the doctor asked I have a nasty cough and a very sore throat I replied

_____

_____

_____

c) What would you like in your lunch box tomorrow Dad asked Please can I have ham sandwiches with tomatoes and crisps I answered Of course you can.

_____

_____

_____

_____

d) Has everyone got a piece of paper Mr Evans asked I haven't I said Don't worry I will get you one he replied.

_____

_____

_____

Paragraphs

Key to punctuation

Paragraphs are groups of sentences that are related to each other. A paragraph often has sentences in it about the same thing or point. A new paragraph is usually started when the writing changes to a new time, action, event, place or person. Usually, a new paragraph starts on a new line and is **indented** (a small gap is left to show that a new paragraph is starting). However, paragraphs are sometimes separated by a **line space** and are not indented.

Indented paragraph

...so snatching up all his things and without stopping to think, Imran bolted out of the door.

   When he got to the end of the lane and could see clearly down the high street, he saw what looked like...

Line-spaced paragraph

... so snatching up all his things and without stopping to think, Imran bolted out of the door.

When he got to the end of the lane and could see clearly down the high street, he saw what looked like...

Practice activities

1. Read the extract below and place a tick where you think a new paragraph could begin.

Little Red Riding Hood skipped out of her house and ran through the forest to her grandma's house. While she was running, she saw some beautiful flowers and stopped to pick some. When she arrived at her grandma's house, she went straight into the bedroom, but something was wrong. Little Red Riding Hood thought her grandma looked very strange today.

2. Look at the basic facts below, which have been taken from a newspaper report. Then make up your own newspaper article using a separate paragraph for each fact.

Animals escaped from the zoo.

The zoo had to close.

The police were called.

_____

_____

_____

_____

_____

_____

_____

_____

_____

_____

_____

_____

_____

_____

_____

_____

_____

_____

_____

Test your punctuation

These questions will help you to practise the punctuation skills you have learned in this book. They will also help you prepare for the grammar and punctuation test that you will take in Year 6 at the end of Key Stage 2.

Make sure you read each question carefully and do what it asks. The questions slowly get harder to help you progress steadily.

1. Draw a line to match each group of words to the correct punctuation mark.

Ouch		?
Where are you		.
I like drinking milk		!

1 mark

2. Add **three** more commas in the right places to make this sentence correct.

    When we went to the farm, I saw cows hens sheep geese and ducks.

1 mark

3. Read the sentences below. Put a circle around any letters that should be **capital letters**, and add the **full stops**.

    a) lisa won first prize in a colouring competition   she was very happy

    b) i love cooking with my mum   when i am older, i would like to be a chef

2 marks

4. Which sentence is punctuated correctly?

    Tick **one**

    Is it Wednesday today? ☐

    Is it Wednesday today. ☐

    Is it Wednesday today! ☐

    Is it Wednesday today, ☐

1 mark

5. Write a **question**.

    _____

1 mark

6. Write an **exclamation**.

_____

1 mark

7. What type of punctuation is another name for **speech marks**?

Tick **one**

commas ☐

exclamation marks ☐

inverted full stops ☐

inverted commas ☐

1 mark

8. Put a circle around the words that should start with a **capital letter**.

a) darcey, elizabeth and tom went to france on a school trip.

1 mark

b) Pick **one** of the words you have circled and explain why it needs a capital letter.

_____

_____

1 mark

9. Add **inverted commas** in the correct place to this sentence.

Is anyone there? shouted Mia.

1 mark

10. Add the **inverted commas** and **correct punctuation** to this conversation.

Can I go and play at Toby's house, please I asked Mum

Mum replied Of course you can

2 marks

11. Give **two** reasons why a new paragraph should be started.

_____

_____

2 marks

Mixed test

These questions give you another chance to practise the grammar and punctuation skills you have learned in this book. They will also help you prepare for the grammar and punctuation test that you will take in Year 6 at the end of Key Stage 2.

Make sure you read each question carefully and do what it asks. The questions slowly get harder to help you progress steadily.

1. Copy the sentence below. Add any missing **full stops** or **capital letters**.

    david hit the ball so hard it smashed a window

    _____

    _____

    1 mark

2. Which sentence contains **two verbs**?

    Tick **one**

    The birds flew in the sky.   ☐

    The birds flew down to their nests.   ☐

    The birds swooped and darted through the sky.   ☐

    The birds collected worms.   ☐   *1 mark*

3. Put a tick in each row to show whether the sentence is a statement or an exclamation.

Sentence	Statement	Exclamation
Ouch, I've hurt my finger!		
I need a plaster.		
My finger is bleeding.		

    1 mark

4. Complete the sentence below with an **adjective** that makes sense.

The _____ sea crashed against the rocks. *1 mark*

5. Complete the table to show the singular and plural forms of each noun.

Singular	Plural
car	
	mice
knife	

1 mark

6. Write either **a** or **an** before each noun.

a) _____ elephant

b) _____ frog *1 mark*

7. Put commas in the correct places to separate the items in the lists.

a) At the weekend I go swimming play football see friends and watch TV.

b) September April June and November all have thirty days.

2 marks

8. Circle the **conjunction** in this sentence.

The children needed a wash because they were dirty. *1 mark*

9. The sentences below are incorrect. Rewrite them correctly.

a) The children was dancing. _____

b) Mike were laughing. _____

2 marks

10. Change this sentence to the **future tense**.

I asked for more.

_____

1 mark

Mixed test

11. Put a circle around the **vowels**.

  s   t   h   a   e   l   m   p   w   i   *1 mark*

12. Write two questions you would like to ask an author.

  a) _____

  b) _____

                                                    2 marks

13. Read the sentence and circle all the **nouns**.

  I like going to the library and choosing new books.   *1 mark*

14. Circle the **adverb** in this sentence.

  The ballerina danced gracefully in her exam this morning.   *1 mark*

15. Write a **different adverb** to change the meaning of the sentence.

  The ballerina danced _____ in her exam this morning.   *1 mark*

16. Add the pronouns **I** and **me** to the sentences below to make them correct.

  Jake and _____ watched his dad wash the car.

  "You splashed _____ !" I shouted.   *2 marks*

17. Choose a **pronoun** from the words below to complete the sentence.

  Aisha went to the shops and _____ bought some ice cream.

  her   **she**   **we**   **it**   **me**   *1 mark*

18. Which **preposition** would fit best in this sentence?

  The car is _____ the garage.

             Tick **one**

  out   ☐

  round   ☐

  over   ☐

  in   ☐

                                                    1 mark

19. Put **inverted commas** in the correct place in the sentences below.

I like your new glasses, Jamie said.

Thank you! replied Michelle.

1 mark

20. Which sentence uses **inverted commas** and **commas** correctly?

Tick **one**

"You shouldn't feed the animals," the zookeeper said. ☐

"You shouldn't feed the animals, the zookeeper said." ☐

"You shouldn't feed the animals" the zookeeper, said. ☐

You shouldn't feed the animals, "the zookeeper said." ☐

1 mark

21. Circle the most suitable connective to complete the sentence below.

Charlie cycled to school this morning _____ usually he walks.

because   **although**   **and**   **next**   *1 mark*

Acknowledgements

The author and publisher are grateful to the copyright holders for permission to use quoted materials and images.

All images are ©Shutterstock, ©Jupiterimages, ©Clipart.com or ©Letts Educational, an imprint of HarperCollins*Publishers* Ltd

Every effort has been made to trace copyright holders and obtain their permission for the use of copyright material. The author and publisher will gladly receive information enabling them to rectify any error or omission in subsequent editions. All facts are correct at time of going to press.

Published by Letts Educational
An imprint of HarperCollins*Publishers* Ltd
1 London Bridge Street
London SE1 9GF

ISBN 9781844198689

First published 2013

This edition published 2015

10 9 8 7 6 5 4 3 2 1

British Library Cataloguing in Publication Data.

A CIP record of this book is available from the British Library.

Commissioning Editor: Tammy Poggo

Author: Laura Griffiths

Project Editors: Daniel Dyer and Charlotte Christensen

Cover Design: Sarah Duxbury

Inside Concept Design: Ian Wrigley

Layout: Jouve India Private Limited

Printed and bound by RR Donnelley APS